Dinosaur Publications

D1742097

Birds in the Garden

by Peter Gill

illustrated by the author

Published by Dinosaur Publications Ltd, Over, Cambridge, England

© Dinosaur Publications Ltd 1981
© text and illustrations Peter Gill 1981

Made in Great Britain

ISBN 0/85122/274/9 (hardback)
ISBN 0/85122/258/7 (paperback)

All gardens are different. Some are small, some are big, some have grass and a pond, some have trees and bushes. Each one has something to please some of the birds in this book.

More birds will come into your garden if you feed them with nuts, seeds, crumbs and fat. Don't feed them in spring or they may carry the wrong food back to their young ones in the nest. They will enjoy drinking and bathing in a bird bath.

Some male (♂) and female (♀) birds look alike but others are quite different.

Where no symbol is given the male and female birds look alike.

Male and female **Robins** look
alike but the young ones have
speckled breasts. They sing
quietly in autumn when other
birds are silent.

The **Missel Thrush** is called
'Storm Cock' because it sings
from the topmost branch of a
windswept tree.

In spring, the **Song Thrush**
lays its beautiful blue eggs
in a mud-lined nest.
It breaks open snail shells
on a favourite stone.

Blackbirds scratch among dead leaves to find food in winter. The female has dark brown feathers and beak.

♂

The **Redwing** visits in winter looking for berries and feeding on the ground when it is not frozen.

The **Fieldfare** is a noisy winter visitor from the north. It eats berries and fallen apples.

House Sparrows always
live near people where
food is easy to find.
The noisy cock sparrow
is a handsome bird
but the hen has paler
colours.

The **Hedge Sparrow** or Dunnock
feeds quietly on the ground
near hedges or bushes.
It eats small seeds
and, in spring, many insects.
Its eggs are beautiful, bright blue.

The **Swift** lives and even sleeps in the air and only comes down to nest under roof tiles or in a hole in a building. Flocks fly screaming among the roof tops before they leave for Africa in autumn.

House Martins build their nests of mud close together under roof eaves. They have white rumps which are easy to see.

The **Swallow** flies each year from South Africa to the same nest in a shed or farm building. It has very long pointed tail feathers.

The **Blue Tit** likes eating nuts. It has also learnt to peck away milk bottle tops to reach the cream.

The **Great Tit** is bigger than the Blue Tit. It steals cream, too, and will use nest boxes put up in the garden.

The **Coal Tit** has a white patch
at the back of its black cap.
It likes woodlands but comes
to bird tables to feed in
winter.

The **Marsh Tit** has no
white patch and does
not come to gardens as
often as the Coal Tit.

The **Starling** cleverly imitates other birds as it sings. Vast flocks gather to roost on buildings and in woods in winter.

Feral Pigeons are descended from pigeons kept in dove-cots for food in olden days. These, in turn, descended from wild Rock Doves.

The **Collared Dove** spread to this country from the East and, although it is a timid bird, it always lives near humans.

The **Wood Pigeon** feeds its young, called squabs, on a milky liquid it makes in its crop. It feeds on grain, young clover and vegetables and can do much damage to farm crops.

The **Goldfinch** has
bright colouring
and a sweet twittering song.
It was often caught and kept
in a cage as a pet but this is
now against the law.

The **Greenfinch** used to be a shy
bird but has learnt to come to
gardens for nuts in the winter.

♂

Chaffinches are more common in winter as local birds are joined by chaffinches from the north.

♂

♀

The **Bullfinch** is lovely to look at but gardeners don't like it because it feeds greedily on young buds of fruit trees, killing some of the fruit.

♂

♀

The **Kingfisher** is usually seen
as a brilliant flash of blue.
It dives into the water
to catch small fish to eat
and to feed its young.
It nests in a tunnel in the
river bank.

The **Moorhen** is a shy bird which flicks
its tail as it tiptoes away. On the
water, it bobs its head as it swims.

The **Heron** may steal
the goldfish from
a garden pool.

The **Treecreeper** starts at the
bottom of a tree, climbing the
trunk as it looks for insects.
When it reaches the top,
it flies to the bottom of the
next tree to start again.

The **Nuthatch** wedges nuts
firmly in cracks in trees so
that it can split the shells
open with its strong beak.

The **Green Woodpecker**
eats insects from tree
trunks and ants on the ground.
It was once called "Yaffle"
after its loud laughing cry.

The **Great Spotted Woodpecker** drums on
tree branches and pecks out a deep hole
for its nest in a rotten tree trunk.

♂

The **Spotted Flycatcher** sits upright on a post or branch and makes quick dashes to catch flying insects.

The **Pied Wagtail** walks about the lawn with its tail wagging and makes sudden dashes after insects. Pied means black and white.

The **Willow Warbler** comes from Africa for the summer. It feeds busily on insects among leaves high in trees and sometimes hovers and darts after flies.

The **Blackcap** is named after the male bird. The female has a brown cap. Most Blackcaps go south for the winter, but some stay and visit bird tables.

♂

The **Goldcrest** is tiny, the
smallest bird in Europe. It builds
its little nest of moss, hair,
feathers and spiders' webs
hanging from the tip of a fir
tree branch.

The **Wren** is small with an
upright tail and a very loud
voice. It builds a domed nest
with a hole in the side, cleverly
hidden among ivy or in a
crevice.

Waxwings come in small
flocks from the far north in
bad winters to feed on
rowan berries and, in gardens,
on cotoneaster and
pyracantha berries.

The **Jackdaw** has a grey cap
and light blue eyes. It nests in
hollow trees and even in chimneys.

Rooks eat many harmful
grubs and insects and
are good friends to
the farmer.

The **Magpie** is very inquisitive and steals small shiny things. It also steals other birds' eggs to feed its young.

The **Jay** hides beechnuts and acorns in the ground to eat in the winter. It forgets where some of them are and they grow into new trees.

The **Barn Owl** is often seen flying like a big white moth in car headlights.

The **Tawny Owl** makes its "Tu-Whit-Tu-Whoo" in winter and early spring. It is difficult to see because it sleeps in daytime in a leafy tree.